The Importance of the Local Church

DANIEL E. WRAY

Pastor of Limington Congregational Church
Limington, Maine

THE BANNER OF TRUTH TRUST

THE BANNER OF TRUTH TRUST
3 Murrayfield Road, Edinburgh EH12 6EL
P.O. Box 621, Carlisle, Pennsylvania 17013, USA

*   *   *

ISBN 0 85151 330 1

TAYLOR, YOUNG (PRINTERS) LTD.
CHELTENHAM

The Importance of the Local Church

It is Saturday evening, and across the land people are again deciding whether or where to attend church services tomorrow. Some will ask themselves: Does church attendance make any difference in the twentieth century? After all, most of us can find a wide variety of religious programmes on radio or television in our homes. Others will go to worship services, but will remain aloof from any serious commitment to the local church they attend. Still others will drift from church to church seemingly unable or unwilling to decide whether they should join one.

It is a time of confusion about the place and purpose of local churches. Christians in by-gone days did not have so many choices with which to contend. They did not have the electronic media, for example. Christian books were neither so plentiful nor so easily obtainable as they are today. Transportation did not allow for the rapid travel which has now become familiar. People could not listen to sermons on tapes as many do so profitably today. The combined effect of these and other present-day circumstances is to encourage contemporary Christians to question the importance of the old-style local church. When one adds to this the many obvious imperfections which are to be found in even the best local churches, the problems and questions increase in intensity.

Are there answers to the questions:

Is the local church important?

Might not Christians get along well without it?

Does it really matter whether I participate in it or not?

Even if I go to church services, does it matter whether I join?

These questions and others should be of great concern to present-day Christians.

In all matters of faith and practice, the Christian has an authoritative guide. The Bible answers the questions and solves the dilemmas which have been proposed above. As we examine the teaching of Holy Scripture, we shall find that our Father in Heaven has not left us to drift about in uncertainty in regard to the place and importance of our membership in a local church.

1. The Glorious Church

The church of the living God from past to present is glorious in his sight. There is no group, no movement, no institution of any kind in the world which can even approach to the glory, the splendour, the honour, the beauty, the magnificence, the wonder, the dignity, the excellence, the resplendency of the church of God. Would to God that we could all be filled to overflowing with a profound sense of the glory of the church as God sees it! Many of our problems about the local church would be solved immediately if we shared God's perspective!

John Newton expressed a measure of this spirit when he paraphrased the teaching of Psalm 87 in his well-known hymn:

Glorious things of thee are spoken, Zion, city of our God;
He whose word cannot be broken formed thee for his own abode:
On the Rock of Ages founded, what can shake thy sure repose?
With salvation's walls surrounded, thou may'st smile at all thy
foes.

But these statements about the glory of God's church are not just romantic illusions. They can be substantiated by the express teaching of Holy Scripture:

1. The glory of the church is seen in her election by God [*Eph* 1.3-6]. Whatever the Lord God has set his purposeful love upon

4

from 'before the foundation of the world' must surely be of paramount importance to him.

2. The glory of the church is seen in the great cost at which she was purchased [*Eph* 1.7, 5.25; I *Pet* 1.18, 19]. We often assess the value of an object by what it cost. God has set the value of his church so high that he sent the 'unspeakable gift' [2 *Cor* 9.15] of his only begotten Son [1 *John* 4.9] to purchase her for himself.

3. The glory of the church is seen in the adoption of her members as children of God [*Eph* 1.5; *Rom* 8.15]. Through the blood of Christ, God not only secured pardon for his people, but also the full standing of children. Furthermore, the church of God is raised to a position of holy royalty. Its people are 'kings and priests unto God' [*Rev* 1.6]. As Peter assures us, the church is 'a royal priesthood, an holy nation' [1 *Pet* 2.9]. This honourable standing before God obviously transcends mere forgiveness. The people of God's church, who were formerly children of wrath and disobedience [*Eph* 2.2, 3; 5.6], are now holy members of the Royal Family of God.

4. The glory of the church is seen also in her splendid and distinguished inheritance [*Eph* 1.14, 18; *Rom* 8.17, 18]. As adopted children, members of God's church are heirs to vast blessings. These include the kingdom of God [*Luke* 12.32], a new heaven and a new earth [2 *Pet* 3.13; *Rev* 21.1], eternal life [*Mark* 10.30; *John* 10.28; *Rom* 6.23; *Heb* 9.15], and the vision of God [*Matt* 5.8]. As the guarantee of these blessings, the Holy Spirit himself has been given as a down-payment [*Eph* 1.13, 14]. Thus the church of God is a company of people called 'into an inheritance that can never perish, spoil or fade — kept in heaven for you, who through faith are shielded by God's power until the coming of the salvation that is ready to be revealed in the last time' [1 *Pet* 1.4, 5 NIV].

5. The glory of the church may be seen in the wonderful purpose and central place she has in the plan of God. God intends to display through the church the glory of his love,

wisdom and grace [*Eph* 1.6, 14, 2.7, 3.10, 11, 21]. Since the church is designated to fulfil such a profound purpose, how can her importance be doubted? She is at the heart of God's plan for his creation [*Eph* 1.9, 10 with 1.22, 23]. Out of the ruins of fallen human nature, God is building a new humanity — the church [*Eph* 2.15, 4.13].

6. The glory of the church is seen in the glory of her Head, the Lord Jesus Christ [*Col* 1.15-19; *Eph* 1.22, 23]. He is supreme above all, and the church participates in his glory as his body [*Eph* 4.15, 16; 5.29, 30]. By virtue of her union with Christ, the church actually participates in 'the fulness of God' [*Eph* 3.19]. The importance of the church cannot be understood apart from the importance of the Lord Jesus Christ. This view of the church's glory is enhanced by a consideration of the great diversity of people which God is forming into the one unified body of Christ [*Eph* 2.11-22; 3.5, 6; *Rev* 7.9; *John* 17.21, 23].

7. The glory of the church may be seen in the fact that she enjoys the personal and powerful ministry of the Holy Spirit [*Eph* 1.13, 14, 17-19, 3.16, 17; *Rom* 8.9-16]. The church (both as individuals and corporately) is the temple of the Holy Spirit [*Eph* 2.21, 22; 1 *Cor* 3.16, 6.19]. Just as the second person of the Holy Trinity became flesh and died to purchase the church, so no less a person than the Holy Spirit of God has come as her indwelling Comforter and Guide [*John* 14.16, 17, 25; 16.13-15].

8. The glory of the church may be seen in her true holiness [*Eph* 1.4; 2.10, 21; 5.26, 27]. Holiness is the true glory and beauty of intelligent moral beings. It is through holy lives that the saints of God's church reflect his image [*Eph* 4.24]. The church is called to a glorious perfection, which consists of nothing less than the imitation of God himself [*Eph* 5.1 cf *Matt* 5.48].

9. The glory of the church may be seen in her nearness and access to God [*Eph* 2.13, 18, 3.12; *Heb* 4.16]. Only the church of God is given such assurance of ready access to the holiest, where God dwells in unapproachable light. Furthermore, Scripture

teaches that God is present with his church [*Eph* 2.22, 5.18; 2 *Cor* 6.16; *Matt* 28.20]. The church lives in present fellowship with him.

10. The glory of the church may be seen in her spiritual knowledge of all the mysteries of the gospel [*Eph* 1.9, 3.2-5; 1 *Cor* 2]. Only the people of God by faith in Jesus Christ have a true spiritual understanding of the things of God. This is so because they have the 'mind of Christ' [1 *Cor* 2.16], and the anointing from God [1 *John* 2.20, 27]. Jesus expressed the church's privilege in this way: 'Henceforth I call you not servants; for the servant knoweth not what his lord doeth: but I have called you friends; for all things that I have heard of my Father I have made known to you' [*John* 15.15].

In the light of all these truths, it is no wonder that Christians with understanding can sing hymns like this:

> *I love thy church, O God!*
> *Her walls before thee stand,*
> *Dear as the apple of thine eye,*
> *And graven on thy hand.*
>
> *For her my tears shall fall,*
> *For her my prayers ascend,*
> *To her my cares and toils be given,*
> *Till toils and cares shall end.*

(Timothy Dwight)

2   *The Visible Glorious Church*

The vision of the church that has been outlined above is so exalted that we might be tempted to consider it very remote from that of the local churches we know. It is certainly the case that all of these truths apply in their perfection only to the church of God as seen from his unclouded perspective.

However, this does not weaken the fact that God has established his glorious church to be visible in the world. God did not light this lamp in order to hide it. The Bible passages already mentioned, which prove how glorious the church is, *were all written to specific local churches*. Such local churches were and are established by God. They are to be visible expressions of the universal glorious church. This can be proved in the following way:

1. The Lord Jesus Christ seldom used the word 'church' in the four Gospels. But when he did use the word, he referred to it as something to be visibly administered upon earth [*Matt* 16.18, 19; 18.15-18]. Furthermore, when the exalted Lord Jesus Christ speaks in Revelation 2 and 3, it is in order to hold particular churches accountable for either spoiling or preserving the glory of his church.

2. In keeping with the Lord's teachings, the apostles established local churches and gave instructions for their continuing maintenance [*Acts* 14.21-23; 1 *Tim* 3.15; *Tit* 1.5]. Are we to consider their practice superfluous?

In the Acts of the Apostles, the word 'church' is used in connection with specific local churches [8.1, 11.22, 26; 13.1; 15.3, 4, 22; 20.17]. This pattern continues in the apostolic letters [1 *Cor* 1.2; 2 *Cor* 1.1; 2 *Thess* 1.1]. These letters also speak in general terms about the 'churches' [*Rom* 16.14; 1 *Cor* 4.17, 7.17, 11.16, 28, 14.33, 16.19]. In all these references, it is obvious that the universal church is locally and visibly expressed in individual church fellowships.

3. This corporate visibility is also evident in what we might call the 'not-alone' passages of the New Testament. These are the passages that show how believers are to relate to 'one another'. The New Testament assumption is that Christians will gather together. They will not try to stay isolated.

The following passages teach us that Christians are expected to relate closely with one another, and that these relationships extend beyond the Lord's Day services: John 13.34, 35;

Romans 12.5, 10, 16, 14.19, 15.14; Galatians 6.2; Ephesians 4.32, 5.21; Philippians 2.3, 4; 1 Thessalonians 4.9, 5.11; Hebrews 10.24; James 5.16; 1 John 4.12. A reading of these verses in their contexts makes clear that the ideals of the glorious church summarized in Section 1 above are being applied to local church life.

These considerations demonstrate the present visibility of God's glorious church. The imperfections evident in every local church do not change the fact that each church is responsible to be a tangible manifestation of the perfect ideal. Furthermore, when the final and universal perfection of the church is reached in the eternal heavenly kingdom, that too will be visible.

3   The Functions of a Biblical Church

A biblical local church provides a ministry which every Christian needs. That is why God's Word issues this command: 'And let us consider one another to provoke unto love and to good works: not forsaking the assembling of ourselves together, as the manner of some is; but exhorting one another: and so much the more, as ye see the day approaching' [*Heb* 10.24, 25]. The necessary functions of a church include:

1. The opportunity for corporate worship and participation in the sacraments of Baptism and the Lord's Supper. Christians can and do worship privately, but public worship is held up to view as necessary, and its practice is assumed, throughout the Bible [*Lev* 23; *Ps* 22.22, 25, 35.18, 107.32, 111.1, 149.1; *Luke* 4.16; *Acts* 2.42, 20.7]. God loves to see his people gathered in public worship. The worship of heaven itself, so far as the Bible gives us a glimpse of it, is worship in a gathered assembly [*Heb* 12.22; *Rev* 5.11-14, 7.9-12, 15.2-4, 19.1-8]. As for the sacraments, they were not given for private use. They are always

corporate ordinances to be observed within the assemblies of God's people. We do not baptize ourselves, nor do we observe the Lord's Supper in isolation.

2. A true local church provides biblical teaching by qualified men sent by God [*Eph* 4.8-11], who are in touch with the needs, the language, and the circumstances of the people whom they serve. Such teaching is necessary for every Christian's healthy development toward spiritual maturity [*Eph* 4.12-14; 1 *Pet* 2.2; *Acts* 20.28-32; 1 *Tim* 3.2; 2 *Tim* 3.16-4.4]. It is vital that qualified and duly-called men be devoted to such work [1 *Tim* 5.17, 4.13-16], and that others attend upon their ministry and support them [1 *Cor* 9.14; *Heb* 13.7, 17; *Col* 4.3].

3. A biblical local church provides opportunity for close Christian fellowship and mutual ministry. The Lord Jesus Christ calls us to a fellowship of inter-dependence in which each part of his body needs the other parts [1 *Cor* 12.13-27; *Eph* 4.16]. Each member is supplied by the Spirit for the profit of the other members [1 *Cor* 12.7]. We need to give more attention to this biblical call to Christian community life. The Holy Spirit desires to transform the Lord Jesus Christ's people from a collection of selfish individuals into a community of self-denying brothers and sisters. The local church is the normal context in which he does this. He was doing this work in the early church [*Acts* 2.42-47]. He continues to do it today.

4. A biblical local church provides the necessary structure and stability to fulfil the New Testament model of a Christian community with sound government and faithful discipline [1 *Tim* 3; *Tit* 1; *Matt* 18.15-17; *Acts* 20.17, 28]. The Lord has not ordained his churches to be unstructured, completely spontaneous, loosely-knit friendship groups. They should rather be like well-managed families. In such well-ordered churches, there will be a healthy mutual responsibility and accountability. This is the God-ordained environment for sanctification and co-operative service. The New Testament metaphors for the church all imply visible order: e.g. 'house' [1

Tim 3.15; *Heb* 3.6]; 'temple' [*Eph* 2.21, 22]; 'fellow-citizens' [*Eph* 2.19f]; 'holy nation' [1 *Pet* 2.9]; 'body' [1 *Cor* 12; *Eph* 4.16].

5. A biblical local church provides the opportunity for co-operative efforts in ministries of mercy and evangelism. Christians are called by the Lord to evangelism [*Matt* 28.18-20; *Acts* 8.4; 1 *Pet* 3.15] and to works of compassion [*Matt* 25.31-46; *Acts* 2.45; 4.32-35; *Gal* 2.10]. Like everything else in the Christian's life, this calling is not a private, individualistic assignment. More can be accomplished when each believer brings his gifts, his resources, his time, and his energy to the task in a harmonious co-operation. When a local church is thus functioning as a healthy, unified and loving community, then the surrounding world profits. Its good fruits will be tasted by many outside itself.

4   Choosing a Church

By now it will be clear that God intends his people to be united together into visible church fellowships. But in case there may be some lingering uncertainty, the following thoughts should be considered:

1. If you want to live in harmony with the mind and heart of God, you must live in love for his church [*Acts* 20.28; *Eph* 5.25]. Anyone who remains aloof from the church of God has spurned the apple of his eye. To fail to desire and work for the advancement of God's church is to be out-of-step with God. We have already seen that God's church is to be visible in the world; therefore our work for the advancement of his universal church must come to tangible expression in work for true local churches. To labour for his churches is to labour for his kingdom, of which they are the present expression [*Matt* 13, 16.18, 19; *Col* 1.13, 4.11].

2. No wise man will say: 'I do not need or want what God has given'. It would simply be pride to think or speak in such a manner! Yet all men who stand aloof from the churches of God set themselves in judgment against the wisdom of God. It is God who established the church and its true local manifestation. Can we ever be justified in treating lightly what he has founded? Furthermore, it is a sin against God and our own souls to deprive ourselves of the blessings and means of grace which God has provided for our good. Yet this is what we do by neglecting the functions of the local church.

3. Consider the overall potential effect of neglecting God's church. If it is right for one to remain aloof and non-committal, then why not two? And if two, why not three; and if three, why not everyone? But if everyone were to do so, where would be the visible witness for the kingdom of God in this crooked and perverse world? It is always good to ask ourselves, when considering any particular course of behaviour: What would happen if everyone thought this way? If we are compelled by such reflection to say: 'It would have very bad effects if everyone neglected the church in the way that I am doing', then we must ask ourselves: 'Then why should I treat myself as an exception?'

4. If we belong to Christ, we belong to one another as members of one body, citizens of one kingdom, brothers and sisters in one household, priests in one temple, soldiers in one army, sheep in one flock. This being so, how can we justify any failure to give visible expression to this great truth? Christians who float around and remain unattached to any one congregation are perhaps inclined to say that they are demonstrating the true spiritual unity of all believers. But is this really so? If unity is displayed simply by talking to one another and by sitting in the same building once in a while, then they are expressing unity. But if true unity always involves a healthy visible commitment to one another, then it is only possible to express the unity Scripture describes by membership in a biblical local church.

Having stressed the importance of local church membership, one final question remains to be considered: How do we choose a biblical church? Indeed this can be a difficult task when one looks around and encounters so many conflicting religious claims. From every direction, we hear the cry: 'Look, Christ is here with us in our church'. Jesus warns us to be alert and careful lest we be deceived by persuasive false teachers [*Matt* 7.15-20, 24.4, 23-25]. Therefore we need to consider the question: 'What criteria are helpful in such an important decision?' The following pointers will provide help in identifying true biblical churches. But it must be realized that they are not intended to sort out all the points of distinction between true churches which differ from one another in some doctrines and practices:

1. Look for a church where there is a strong emphasis on Bible teaching and the application of biblical teaching to daily life. The local church should follow the model of the apostles who taught *both* objective truth, and *also* how believers were to live from day to day. For example, compare Ephesians, chapters 1-3, with chapters 4-6. A pastor should be 'apt to teach' [1 *Tim* 3.2], and should labour in this work [1 *Tim* 5.7; 2 *Tim* 3.16-4.4]. Look for a church where the pastor does this. Avoid a church that has given this work over to women, contrary to the New Testament's clear teaching [1 *Tim* 2.12; 2 *Tim* 2.2].

2. Look for a church where worship is reverent and biblical. Beware of churches that entertain people more than they worship God, and which introduce elements into worship which are not taught in the Bible. The basic elements of true worship are: Prayer [*Matt* 6.9-13; *Acts* 2.42, 4.23-31]; reading and exposition of Scripture [1 *Tim* 4.13; 2 *Tim* 4.2; *Eph* 4.11, 12]; singing [*Matt* 26.30; *Eph* 5.18-20; *Col* 3.16]; offerings [1 *Cor* 16.1, 2; 2 *Cor* 8 and 9; *Prov* 3.9; *Phil* 4.18]; confessions of faith [1 *Cor* 15.3-5; *Rom* 10.9, 10]; the Lord's Supper [*Matt* 26.17; 1 *Cor* 11.23-29]; and Baptism [*Matt* 28.19; *Acts* 2.38]. Seek a church where these elements are given full attention, without

being pushed to the side by other things.

3. Look for a church where the 'love of the brethren' is evident [*John* 13.34, 35, 15.9-12; *Eph* 4.29-5.2; 1 *John* 4.7-5.2]. This, of course, is not something which is always readily visible to the occasional visitor. Remember that such love grows in the environment of a commitment to a local church, and it manifests itself in actions as well as words.

4. Look for a church where discipline is practised in accordance with Scripture [*Matt* 18.15-17; 1 *Cor* 5]. (See my booklet, *Biblical Church Discipline* for details).

5. Look for a church which demonstrates the Lord's compassion for the lost by works of evangelism and mercy [*Matt* 9.36-38, 14.14; *Mark* 6.34; *Luke* 10.25-37].

6. You are duty-bound not to affiliate with any church which denies any of the fundamental doctrines of the Christian faith, such as are summarized (for example) in the Apostles' Creed or the Nicene Creed; and in such passages as Romans 1.1-6, 1 Corinthians 15.3-5. The churches of Christ are clearly responsible to uphold God's truth; therefore this is a vital criterion when choosing a church [see 1 *Tim* 3.15; 2 *Tim* 1.13, 14, 2.2; *Jude* 3]. A true church will place a strong emphasis upon the importance of truth.

On the other hand, let us remember that love for the truth should not exist in isolation from love for people, especially those of the household of faith [*Gal* 6.10]. Sometimes one will encounter churches which are strict in their adherence to theological orthodoxy, while neglecting love and works of evangelism and mercy (as mentioned in paragraphs 3 and 5). Seek a church which is trying to practise all of these virtues together. We should be as zealous for love and mercy as we are for truth, and *vice versa*.

7. Recognize that there is no such thing as a perfect local church. Neither the pastor, nor the other officers, nor the people can be expected to please you in every particular. Nor should you be surprised to find inconsistencies even in good

Other booklets in this series:

churches. As churches are made up of imperfect people, so these imperfections and deficiencies will appear in the church's life. One must not become hyper-critical in choosing a church. This principle also applies to how you use second-hand information about a church. Be careful about your sources of information. They may not be reliable. True churches are sometimes badly maligned.

These principles attempt to apply what was said under Section 3 about the functions of a true church. If you find one fulfilling that biblical description, you have found a good church. If you find more than one such church in your area, then you must needs apply additional factors in making your choice. But do make a choice; and do so without disrupting the churches you are considering. Proceed prayerfully and patiently, and God will direct you.

5 Conclusion

One of the greatest needs of our times is for living, biblical churches. No other institutions can adequately replace them. Every Christian ought to give much thought and prayer to this subject, and then order his life in such a way as to further the work of God's true churches. This is not a time for an apathetic, easy-going attitude toward churches. The needs are great. The pressures of ungodliness are heavy. Those who demean God's churches are legion. Let us, then, rise up and go forth with boldness to declare ourselves servants of the God and Father of our Lord Jesus Christ, by following his will in his local church wherever his providence directs us.